Saving the Prairie Bandit

Dorothy Hinshaw Patent

A Wildlife Conservation Society Book

Franklin Watts
A Division of Scholastic Inc.
New York • Toronto • London • Auckland • Sydney
Mexico City • New Delhi • Hong Kong
Danbury, Connecticut

The Wildlife Conservation Society (WCS) is dedicated to protecting
and promoting the world's wildlife and wilderness areas. Founded in
1895 as the New York Zoological Society, the organization operates
the Bronx Zoo, New York Aquarium, Central Park Wildlife Center,
Queens Wildlife Center, and Prospect Park Wildlife Center. WCS
also operates St. Catherine's Wildlife Center, which is located off the
coast of Georgia. The scientists at this center raise and study a variety
of threatened and endangered animals.

WCS currently sponsors more than 350 field projects in 52
countries. The goal of these projects is to save wild landscapes and the
animals that depend on them. In addition, WCS's pioneering environ-
mental education programs reach more than 3 million students in the
New York metropolitan area and are used in all 50 states and 14
foreign nations.

The author wishes to thank Randy Matchett,
Mike Lockhart, Tim Clark, Steve Martin, and
Tom Thorne for their help with this book.

Library of Congress Cataloging-in-Publication Data

Patent, Dorothy Hinshaw.
    Saving the prairie bandit / by Dorothy Hinshaw Patent
        p. cm.— Wildlife conservation society books
    Includes bibliographical references.
    ISBN 0-531-11851-7 (lib. bdg.)   0-531-16567-1 (pbk.)
        1. Black-footed ferret—Juvenile literature. [1. Black-footed ferret. 2. Ferret.
3. Endangered species.] I. Title.

QL737.C25 P288 2001
599.76'629—dc21

                                                          00-051350

Contents

Meet the Author

Dorothy likes to experience what she writes about firsthand. Here, she holds a captive red wolf puppy while researching her book, Gray Wolf, Red Wolf.

Dorothy Hinshaw Patent was born in Minnesota and grew up in California. She has loved animals from the time she was a girl. She studied biology at Stanford University, where she earned a B.A. Then she received an M.A and a Ph.D. from the University of California, Berkeley. She now lives in Missoula, Montana, with her husband and two dogs.

"I began writing in 1972, when my children were young," says Dorothy. "Over the years, I have written more than 100 books, but I still remember working on my very first one. It was about the about the weasel family, which includes the black-footed ferret. Maybe that's one reason I have a special fondness for ferrets.

"In recent years, I've become interested in the North American prairies and their abundant plant and animal life. I have written a number of books about

The black-footed ferret has the typical shape of a member of the weasel family.

prairie ecosystems. When the opportunity came to write a book about black-footed ferrets, I was delighted.

"The first thing I did was plan a trip to see wild ferrets at the UL Bend National Wildlife Refuge in Montana. My "tour guide" was wildlife biologist Randy Matchett. Years ago, I saw ferrets in *captivity* at the Sybille Wildlife Research and Conservation Education Center near Wheatland, Wyoming. At that time, some ferrets had been released, but no one knew whether they could ever live successfully in the wild. I am happy that there are now several hundred black-footed ferrets living on prairie land in the United States. Many scientists have worked hard to make this happen. We owe them all a great debt."

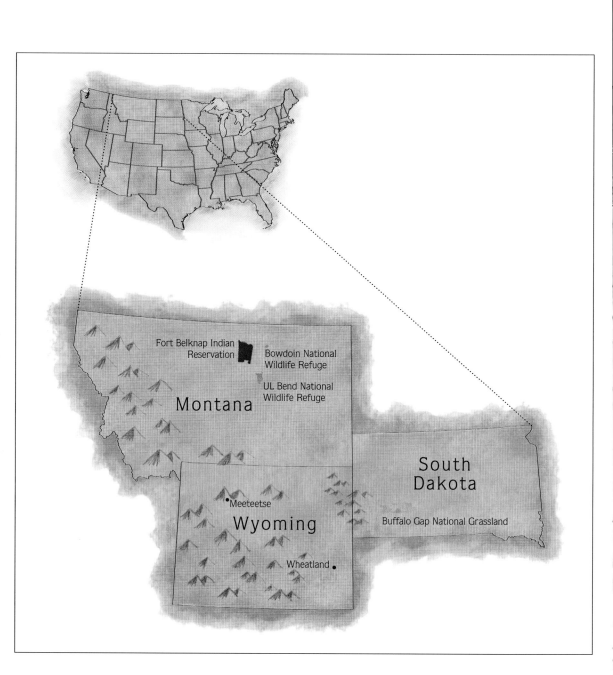

Dorothy has received numerous awards and honors for her work, including the Eva Gordon Award from the American Nature Study Society and the

Randy Matchett is often away from his family for days at a time, so he's happy when they can join him. In this photo, Randy and his children, Sam and Maggie, are ready to release a black-footed ferret. They are wearing masks so they will not spread germs to the ferret.

Golden Kite from the Society of Children's Book Writers and Illustrators. You can learn more about Dr. Patent and her work by visiting her web site at *www.dorothyhinshawpatent.com.*

Although some black-footed ferrets now live in the wild again, they are still seriously endangered.

Chapter 1

Nighttime Adventure

It's a pitch-black night at the end of July. For the last 4 hours, Randy Matchett and I have been bumping along the rutted roads at UL Bend National Wildlife Refuge in Montana. We are looking for black-footed ferrets—one of the most endangered mammals in North America.

Randy is one of many wildlife biologists working to save black-footed ferrets. About 20 years ago, scientists thought these ferrets had all died out, but then they found a few survivors. They worked hard to raise black-footed ferrets at special *breeding centers*—and succeeded. Some ferrets have now been released into the wild. We are hoping to see some ferrets tonight.

Randy knows exactly how to find wild ferrets. As he steers his truck with one hand, he uses the

This back-footed ferret has been raised in captivity. Perhaps one day it will be released into the wild.

other to sweep a powerful beam of light across the prairie. Now and then, the light picks up some *eye shine* from an animal on the prowl. A coyote's eyes shine yellow-green. A rabbit's eyes shine red. We are looking for the brilliant, emerald-green eye shine of a black-footed ferret.

I'm starting to fight sleep when, suddenly, we see what we have been looking for—green eye shine. As we drive closer, the ferret disappears below ground. It is hiding in a prairie dog's burrow.

The green eye shine of a black-footed ferret is easy to spot.

We hop out of the truck and walk over the muddy prairie toward the hole.

As we approach, the curious ferret peeks out several times. When we are just a few feet away, the ferret pops up and looks right at us. Even the flash of my camera doesn't disturb it much. I can't believe I'm finally seeing a black-footed ferret in the wild!

We return to the truck, and Randy continues to flash his light across the prairie. Suddenly, we see the eye shine of another black-footed ferret. It is a young one—a 2-month-old kit. The first ferret we saw is the kit's mother. Now the female runs toward her baby, and they quickly disappear into a hole. A moment later, both ferrets peek out. All we can see are two bobbing pairs of green glowing circles.

Suddenly, another set of eyes appears next to the mother's. Now we know she has at least two kits. The ferrets keep popping up and

Black-footed ferrets are curious animals, and they feel safe as long as we don't get too close.

down. We keep watching and waiting. After a few minutes, four pairs of bright green spots pop out of the same hole. They are all kits. Randy is delighted.

Spotting a Prairie Bandit

The black-footed ferret gets its nickname, "the prairie bandit," from the black mask across its face. Along with its black legs and black tail tip, this mask makes the prairie bandit an appealing creature. A ferret's sides are yellowish-tan, and its back and the top of its head are brown.

Although a female ferret may give birth to as many as six young, it is unusual for so many to survive.

Now all the young ferrets scamper out of their hole. They are about half the size of their mother. The kits wriggle and bound on the ground. Their mother arches her flexible back into an upside down "U." She faces one kit and hops toward it and then away from it with tiny bouncy steps. The youngster doesn't seem to know that its mother wants to play.

I'm completely entranced, and I could watch these ferrets forever. But Randy gently says, "Shall we go find another family? We know where these are, and there's always tomorrow night."

I suddenly remember that we are supposed to be trying to find as many ferret families as we can. Last year, researchers spotted fifteen or sixteen families with a total of forty-one kits. They hope to find more this year, and so far we are off to a good start.

Chapter 2

Bringing Back the Ferret

Researchers at UL Bend National Wildlife Refuge stay in small trailers next to a prairie-dog town.

The next morning, I wake up at 8:20 A.M. and look around my tiny trailer. It is my temporary home at UL Bend National Wildlife Refuge. I have been asleep for only 3 hours, but I'm wide awake. After fixing my breakfast, I eat it at a picnic table outside. Behind me is a row of trailers where researchers can stay and an old cabin where equipment is stored. This is "ferret camp."

The camp is surrounded by dozens of burrow holes. They are the telltale signs that the tunnels of a prairie-dog "town" lie just below the ground. Now

Black-tailed prairie dogs are the main source of food for black-footed ferrets.

and then, I hear a black-tailed prairie dog belt out a warning bark as a hawk flies overhead.

Why is a "ferret camp" surrounded by a prairie-dog community? Black-footed ferrets rarely eat anything other than prairie dogs, and black-footed ferrets live in their burrows. Ferrets can only survive in places where there are plenty of prairie dogs.

As I eat breakfast, I think about black-footed ferrets. Not long ago, they were nearly *extinct*. They were dying out because people were killing prairie dogs and destroying prairies to build farms and towns. Without prairie dogs to eat and prairie-dog burrows to live in, the black-footed ferret was doomed in the wild.

What Happened to Prairie Dogs?

Before Europeans began to settle in the American West, prairie dogs lived throughout the mixed grass and short grass prairies that covered the middle of the North American continent. In 1900, almost 700 million acres (283 million hectares) of prairie-dog

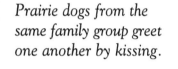

Prairie dogs from the same family group greet one another by kissing.

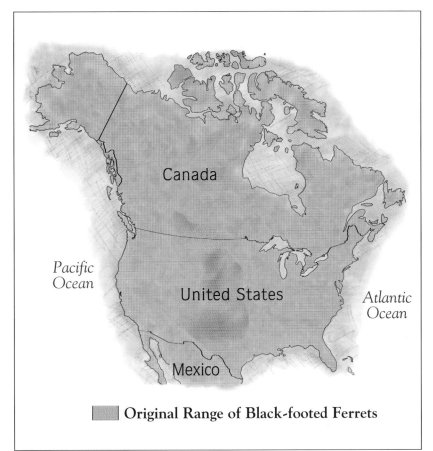

Canada

Pacific
Ocean

United States

Atlantic
Ocean

Mexico

■ **Original Range of Black-footed Ferrets**

habitat stretched from Alberta and Saskatchewan in Canada into northern Mexico. They covered most of the states of North Dakota, South Dakota, Nebraska, Kansas, and Oklahoma. They also covered large areas of Montana, Colorado, Wyoming, New Mexico, and Texas and small areas of Arizona and Utah. Trapping records and information from Indian tribes show that black-footed ferrets occurred over nearly the same range as three species of prairie dogs.

Beginning in the late 1800s, farmers began to plow under huge areas of prairie, leaving only 5 to 10 percent of the original land where prairie dogs lived. Cattle ranchers thought prairie dogs were competing with their animals for food, so they began to poison the prairie dogs. Millions of prairie dogs lost their lives. By 1960, prairie dogs probably existed on only 2 percent of the habitat they had lived on before 1870. The remaining *colonies* were relatively small and widely scattered.

As prairie dogs died, so did black-footed ferrets. Between 1946 and 1953, people reported seeing only about seventy ferrets. About one-third of the animals were found dead. By the early 1960s, most scientists thought ferrets were extinct.

Ferrets—Found and Lost and Found Again

In 1964, something surprising happened. A researcher found a colony of black-footed ferrets in South Dakota. But scientists soon realized that the colony was in trouble. The ferrets would not survive much longer. The scientists took five of the ferrets into captivity, but the animals did not produce young. When the last ferret died in 1979, most people were sure that they were gone forever.

Shep (center) and a friend take a rest on the ranch owned by John and Lucille Hogg. Shep has become famous to people who study black-footed ferrets.

Then, in September 1981, a dog named Shep brought an unusual dead animal to his owners. John and Lucille Hogg lived on a ranch near Meeteetse, Wyoming. John threw away the dead animal, but Lucille was curious. She retrieved the strange-looking creature and took it to an animal expert. He knew the animal was a black-footed ferret and notified wildlife authorities.

At a town meeting called soon after, a ranch worker said he'd seen one of these animals on another ranch. The search was on.

Steve Martin setting up a ferret trap near Meeteetse, Wyoming

At 6:20 A.M. on October 29, wildlife biologists Steve Martin and Denny Hammer saw an amazing sight. Their lights picked up eye shine that glowed like two priceless emeralds. There was a black-footed ferret! The men yelled and cried out with joy. Then they captured the ferret and put a radio collar on it. They wanted to be able to track the animal. From then on, scientists studied the Meeteetse ferret colony closely.

By 1984, the colony had a total of 129 ferrets. The next year, prairie dogs in the area became

Keeping Up Hope

In the mid-1960s, Tim Clark was studying prairie dogs and became interested in black-footed ferrets. He started looking for them in 1973. "I looked for a year, all the time," says Tim. "I lived in Wyoming, and my guess was that they still survived there. Over the next 8 years, I sent out 10,000 postcards offering a reward to anyone who found a ferret."

When ferrets were found near Meeteetse, Wyoming, Clark surveyed other prairie-dog towns in the area. "After the ferrets died out in Wyoming," adds Tim, "I spent another 5 or 6 years looking in Montana. Even though I never found any ferrets, I had fun. I was outdoors camping by myself at least 100 nights a year. I learned a lot about ferrets and prairie dogs, and the ranch folks became very good friends."

WANTED

DO NOT KILL OR TRAP

DO NOT KILL OR TRAP

$50 REWARD
for Photograph & Information

REWARD CONDITIONS: The ferret is an endangered species and is protected by very stringent federal and state laws. The reward WILL NOT be paid for any ferret caught in traps or killed by the finder. The reward will be given to the FIRST person providing information leading to the discovery and verification of the existence of black-footed ferrets (Mustela nigripes) in Wyoming. Skins and skeletons of ferrets struck accidently by cars and found along roads, reports of ferrets seen or photographs taken in an area where a representative of the "Ferret Search" project subsequently observes a ferret will qualify for the reward. A few ferrets have been seen in most parts of Wyoming in recent years. Ferrets eat prairie dogs and are usually found on or near prairie dog towns.

IDENTIFYING CHARACTERISTICS: The ferret is the size of a medium sized mink, about 18 inches long and 2.5 pounds. Unique features are black face mask and black feet. Do not confuse it with long-tailed weasels (no mask or black feet).

CONTACT: Tim W. Clark, Ferret Search, Box 1330, Jackson, Wyoming 83001; Telephone: 307-733-4806 as soon as possible after the sighting.

"Ferret Search" supported by National Geographic Society and The National Academy of Sciences. Reward offer expires 1 November, 1975.

infected with a deadly disease called *sylvatic plague*. As the number of prairie dogs fell, so did the number of ferrets. Eventually, all the prairie dogs and ferrets died out.

Today, *several breeding centers in the United States and Canada use the method developed at Sybille to encourage adult ferrets to mate and produce kits.*

Ferrets in Captivity

Before the Meeteetse ferret colony died out, researchers captured the remaining eighteen healthy animals. They were taken to the Sybille Wildlife Research and Conservation Education Center near Wheatland, Wyoming. The scientists there discovered how to encourage seven of the ferrets to breed and raise their young successfully. Those seven ferrets are the ancestors of all known black-footed ferrets today.

I visited the Sybille captive breeding center in 1995. By that time, a few hundred ferrets were living at seven breeding facilities in the United States and Canada. Scientists had been releasing ferrets into the wild for about 5 years. The program at UL Bend Refuge had been underway for a year.

Before I was allowed to see the ferrets at the breeding center, I had to get very clean. In the past, diseases had brought near-disaster to the ferrets. No one wanted that to happen again. First I had to take a shower and wash my hair. Then I entered a room with an assortment of dark-blue coveralls. I found a pair that fit and struggled into them. Then I chose a pair of thongs for my feet. I was finally ready to meet the ferrets.

It was feeding time. As I passed each cage, the animal inside rose on its back legs and sniffed the air. It wanted to know whether I had any food. I

This black-footed ferret is ready for its dinner.

didn't, but the woman who would feed them wasn't far behind. Using an ice-cream scoop, she doled out each animal's meal—a pile of dark-red ground meat.

As soon as the food appeared, each ferret snapped up a mouthful and scurried down its artificial tunnel to its nest box below. After stashing the food, it returned for more. When the pile was gone, the ferret disappeared to feed in the dark safety of its nest. As the feeding ended, the sound of tiny claws scratching on plywood cage floors gradually subsided. Then there was silence.

Tom Thorne (right) poses with Louise Richardson-Forest and a black-footed ferret.

Tricks of the Trade

That is when my guide, veterinarian Tom Thorne, began to tell me what it is like to work with ferrets. Black-footed ferrets are secretive, sensitive animals. They often appear nervous, and they are easy to upset.

Getting ferrets to breed in captivity is a challenge. Since only seven animals made up the founding stock of all the black-footed ferrets alive today, matings must be carefully arranged to reduce

Working with Ferrets

When a ferret needs to be examined or moved from one place to another, researchers gently coax it into a small wire cage. To a ferret, the close walls of the wire cage feel similar to its underground home. This helps reduce the stress of being handled.

inbreeding as much as possible. Inbreeding, or mating of closely related individuals, can result in a variety of health problems.

The male is put into the female's nest box for two to three nights in a row. Then biologists check to make sure that the female is pregnant. After about 6 weeks, scientists clean her cage thoroughly. Then they leave the ferret alone. They also stay away from nearby cages during this critical period.

Like mating, birth usually takes place at night. A female usually has a *litter* of one to six young. Each tiny kit weighs about as much as two quarters and is covered with a thin coat of fine white hair. Its eyes are closed, and its ears are flattened against

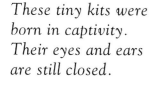

These tiny kits were born in captivity. Their eyes and ears are still closed.

These black-footed ferret kits are about 2 months old. They like to stay together in a cozy nest box.

its head. The babies huddle together in a tangled-up fuzzy ball to nap.

Their teeth begin to come in when they are about 2 weeks old, and soon their fur starts to darken. By 6 weeks of age, their eyes and ears are open. After a few more days, the young ferrets start to walk. Scientists have learned that kits come to prefer the food they eat when they are 8 to 14 weeks old. During that time, researchers make sure the kits eat only prairie-dog meat.

Raising young ferrets in captivity is difficult. A roomful of caged ferrets is very different from the dark peace and quiet of an underground burrow. Even with the best possible care, many kits die.

Getting Ready for the Prairie

On our way to the UL Bend Refuge, Randy Matchett and I stopped at Bowdoin National Wildlife Refuge in Malta, Montana. He wanted to show me the outdoor pens used to prepare ferrets for life in the wild.

These pens at the Bowdoin National Wildlife Refuge in Malta, Montana, give ferrets a chance to live outdoors before they are released into the wild.

When the doors of the white nest box are closed, it can be pulled out of the ground and carried to a ferret release site.

If the ferrets have some experience living outdoors and using prairie-dog burrows for shelter, they have a better chance of surviving. Growing kits also learn how to hunt and kill prairie dogs while they are in the pens. Ferrets need to be skilled hunters before they are released into the wild.

Randy opened the gate of the wire-mesh fence and stooped low to get into one of the pens. I followed. He removed a heavy metal cover to show me the underground nest boxes where the ferrets breed and give birth. When closed, the nest boxes are dark, but the biologists can open them if necessary. When it's time to transport a ferret to its new home in the wild, its nest box can be removed with the ferret inside.

The most dangerous time for the ferrets in the wild is right after they are released. Until they learn where the burrow entrances are, they are easy *prey* for coyotes and badgers. To help the ferrets, Randy has developed a system of electric fences that is used to keep *predators* temporarily away from newly released ferrets.

But even with the help of biologists, many ferrets die before they can raise families the following year.

Those that survive, however, teach their young to live in the wild. Kits born in the wild have a very good chance of surviving and producing families of their own.

Randy checks on a ferret. During the late summer and fall, he often works night and day.

Working with Ferrets

Black-footed ferrets spend most of their lives underground. They mate, give birth, raise their young, and hunt in prairie-dog burrows. Biologists who study ferrets have to work at night, when ferrets come aboveground for a short time.

When I ask Randy about his schedule, he says, "I have dinner and sleep for a couple of hours. Then I go out and look for ferrets. When the sun comes up, I return to camp and sleep until 11:00 or so. Then I eat a big breakfast. After I've been doing this for a couple of weeks, I sometimes sleep 14 hours straight when I get home. I always sleep a lot when I first get home—much to the disgust of my wife and kids!"

Randy does most of his ferret fieldwork in the late summer and autumn. Our late July scouting trip is the first time Randy has looked for ferrets this year. The kits are just getting old enough to spend some time aboveground. Mother ferrets move their kits from one burrow to another, often taking them to a prairie dog she has killed. By late August, when

Black-footed Ferrets: The Facts

SCIENTIFIC NAME:	*Mustela nigripes*, a member of the weasel family
FOOD:	Mostly prairie dogs, sometimes mice, ground squirrels, rabbits, birds
BODY LENGTH:	20 to 24 inches (51 to 61 centimeters), including a 5- to 6-inch (13- to 15-cm) tail
WEIGHT:	$1\frac{1}{2}$ to $2\frac{1}{2}$ pounds (0.6 to 1.1 kilograms); males are slightly bigger than females
LIFESPAN:	About 1 to 4 years in the wild; 9 years in captivity
LOCATION:	Originally lived in most of the mixed and short grass prairies of North America; now they live only in captivity and at a few reintroduction sites in Arizona, South Dakota, Montana, Wyoming, Colorado, and Utah
POPULATION	350 to 400 in captivity; 300 to 350 at reintroduction areas

the kits are about 12 weeks old, their mothers start to take them along on hunts.

"In September, we really get to work," says Randy. "By then, we hope we've counted all the kits and know who their mothers are. We trap the kits and give them shots of *vaccine* that can protect them from diseases. We also place *transponder tags* under their skin. One goes in their neck, and a backup

Randy has just trapped this black-footed ferret (left). This scientist is tracking the movements of black-footed ferrets (below).

goes under the skin near their hip. Since each ferret has its own unique tag, we can identify each animal and find out where it goes. We can also keep track of the kits from each litter. That way we know how all the ferrets are related to one another."

Finding a New Home

In early fall, young ferrets leave their mother to find their own home *territories*. When prairie dogs were common across the middle of North America, finding a new home wasn't hard for a young ferret. Today, the remaining prairie-dog colonies are small and scattered—with cities, farms, and ranches separating

Prairie dogs need open land to build their towns.

them. This makes it very difficult for a young ferret to find a place to settle down. If a young ferret can't find a territory, it won't survive.

An average ferret family eats about 750 prairie dogs a year. To catch this much food, a female ferret needs about 100 acres (40.5 ha) of black-tailed prairie-dog town.

Before scientists decide where to release ferrets, they must think about predators, such as coyotes, badgers, and even great horned owls. They must also think carefully about how the animals will survive over time. Researchers agree that a healthy ferret colony should have at least 100 females. That means they need a site with at least 10,000 acres (4,050 ha) of prairie-dog town.

Unfortunately, no more than five locations in North America have that much habitat today. So even

These black-footed ferrets live in one of the prairie-dog towns at UL Bend National Wildlife Refuge.

though UL Bend Refuge has only 2,000 to 3,000 acres (810 to 1,214 ha) of prairie-dog towns, scientists decided to start a release program there. Today, it is the second most successful reintroduction site in the United States.

A colony at Buffalo Gap National Grassland in South Dakota is doing even better. One reason for its success is that the ferrets have 8,000 to 10,000 acres (3,240 to 4,050 ha) of high-quality, continuous prairie-dog town to live on. The area is chock-full of healthy prairie dogs. These animals are producing wild kits that are being moved to other sites.

Into the Future

The prairie dogs and ferrets at both UL Bend and Buffalo Gap seem very healthy. Still, Randy is worried. He talks about his concerns as we sit at the picnic table. We are looking out over the colony of fat, alert black-tailed prairie dogs.

"What you see here could disappear in 10 days," Randy says. "A disease is killing off prairie dogs at

Healthy prairie dogs like these can quickly die of sylvatic plague.

A coyote will kill any black-footed ferret it can catch. Coyotes can also spread sylvatic plague, a disease that kills ferrets.

Fort Belknap Indian Reservation, which isn't far away. Other prairie-dog colonies within 10 miles of here have died out within the last 2 months. That could be the end of ferret recovery in Montana."

It's hard for me to believe these healthy animals could be so easily wiped out, but I know he's right. The disease Randy is talking about is called sylvatic plague. It is the same disease that killed ferrets and prairie dogs at Meeteetse. The disease is carried by fleas and can be spread quickly and easily by many animals, including coyotes.

Luckily, the ferret recovery program continues to expand. Hopefully, the ferrets at these new sites will live. Then, even if the Montana ferrets die of the

A scientist releases a black-footed ferret at a site in Arizona.

plague, there will still be other black-footed ferrets in the wild.

So far, ferrets have been released in six states—Arizona, Colorado, Montana, South Dakota, Utah, and Wyoming. But there's still a long way to go. The goal of the black-footed ferret recovery plan is to establish at least ten wild populations totaling 1,500 or more breeding animals by the year 2010. Meanwhile, a breeding population of at least 240 animals will remain in captivity.

"The trouble is," says Randy, "we're trying to recover ferrets in the exact same environment that caused them to die. We no longer have the original prairie with bison, wolves, and lots of prairie dogs. Now we have a very fragmented prairie with small, isolated towns."

Disease, poisoning, and prairie-dog shooting, as well as land development, threaten the prairie-dog

As long as people kill prairie dogs and destroy the land they live on, black-footed ferrets will be in danger too.

colonies that still remain. The only way to bring back the black-footed ferret and be confident it will survive is to restore large areas of intact prairie and stop killing prairie dogs. Ferrets aren't the only animals that would benefit. Many kinds of prairie life are disappearing fast, and a lot of work remains to be done to save them.

In 1998, the National Wildlife Federation asked the U.S. Fish and Wildlife Service to list the black-tailed prairie dog as a threatened species. The Fish and Wildlife Service agreed that prairie dogs need help, but so many other species were—and still are—in trouble that it decided not to list the black-tailed prairie dog yet.

Meanwhile, across the remaining prairies, conservation organizations and government agencies are devoting their attention and their money to conserving the prairie and the creatures that live there. Several organizations are also working to restore damaged prairies to their former health. Hopefully, there will be enough healthy prairie in the future to support all the animals that depend on these beautiful grasslands. Only then will the black-footed ferret survive.

Like prairie dogs and ferrets, buffalo need large areas of grasslands to survive.

Important Words

breeding center   (noun) a place where animals are taken into captivity to mate and produce young

captivity   (noun) An animal taken into captivity lives in a pen or cage. It is kept in captivity so that people can see it or scientists can study it.

colony   (noun) a group of animals that live together in one area

eye shine   (noun) the bright reflection from the eyes of animals at night

extinct   (noun) having died out, disappearing from Earth forever

habitat   (noun) the place where a living thing normally can be found

inbreeding   (noun) the mating of closely related individuals

litter	(noun) a group of young born at the same time to the same mother
predator	(noun) an animal that hunts and kills other animals for food
prey	(noun) an animal that predators hunt for food
sylvatic plague	(noun) a disease that kills prairie dogs and ferrets
territory	(noun) the place where an animal lives, feeds, mates, and raises young
transponder tag	(noun) a tiny device that sends out a signal. It is placed under an animal's skin so that scientists can track its movements.
vaccine	(noun) a substance that causes an animal's body to form protective chemicals against the germs that cause a particular disease

To Find Out More

Books and Magazine Articles

Chadwick, Douglas and Jim Brandenberg, photographer. "The American Prairie: Roots of the Sky." *National Geographic* (October 1993): 90–119.

Clark, Tim W. and Franz J. Camenzind, photographer. "Last of the Black-Footed Ferrets?" *National Geographic* (June 1983): 828–838.

Line, Les. "Phantom of the Plains: North America's Black-Footed Ferret." *Wildlife Conservation* (August 1997): 20–27.

Patent, Dorothy Hinshaw. *Prairie Dogs*. New York: Clarion Books, 1993.

_____. *Prairies*. New York: Holiday House, 1996.

Silverstein, Alvin, Virginia Silverstein, and Laura Silverstein Nunn. *The Black-Footed Ferret*. Brookfield, CT: Millbrook Press, 1995.

Vergoth, Karin and Christopher Lampton. *Endangered Species*. Danbury, CT: Franklin Watts, 1999.

Organizations and Online Sites

Black-Footed Ferret Recovery Implementation Team

http://www.blackfootedferret.org

This site features ferret facts, up-to-date information about efforts to protect and save black-footed ferrets, and a description of their prairie habitat.

National Wildlife Federation Prairie Dog Home Page

http://www.nwf.org/prairiedogs/index.html

This Web page has many links to information about grasslands, prairie dogs, and their importance.

Nebraska National Forest Black-Footed Ferret Page

http://www.fs.fed.us/r2/nebraska/gpng/black_footed_ferret.html

Black-footed ferrets may be reintroduced into Nebraska at some future date. This site features up-to-date information about ferrets and the recovery programs in other states.

Society for the Protection and Conservation of the Black-Footed Ferret

http://www.acmeferret.com/saveBFFs/

This site has links, a list of books, and a lot of information about black-footed ferrets.

Wildlife Conservation Society

http://www.wcs.org

2300 Southern Blvd.

Bronx, NY 10460-1099

This organization is dedicated to saving wild landscapes and the creatures that depend on them.

Index

Photographs ©: Corbis-Bettmann: 5 (D. Robert Franz), 41 (Jeff Vanuga); Dembinsky Photo Assoc./Dominique Braud: 39 bottom; Dorothy H. Patent: backcover, 1, border art, 14 bottom, 30, 32; Jeff Vanuga: cover; Louis R. Hanebury: 19, 20, 21, 25, 35; M. R. Matchett: 7, 10, 11, 12, 29, 38; Peter Arnold Inc.: 8 (Steve Kaufman), 42 (Gerard Lacz), 36, 37 (Gunter Ziesler); Photo Researchers, NY/Wm. Munoz: 9 bottom, 28; Photodisc, Inc.: backcover, 9 top, 14 top, 23, 39 top, 44, 45; Visuals Unlimited/John C. Muegge: 40; Wm. Munoz: 15, 16, 22, 24, 26, 27, 43.